PART-TIME WEALTH

BY T.J. ROHLEDER

How to Make Huge Sums of Money in as Little as 90 Days.

Take a Guru to Lunch
P.O. Box 198
Goessel, Kansas 67053

ISBN 1-933356-56-1

INTRODUCTION

Thank you for reading this small book. As you will (hopefully) see, this can change your life. That's a tall order. I know. But keep an open mind and read closely.

By the time you're done going through this small book, you'll have all the secrets for how and why our System can help you make all the money you want, need, and deserve. All from home.

Does that sound like hype?

Well, it's not! By the time you're done reading this small book, (and going to Audible.com and listening to the audio book that this small book is based on).

Don't let the size of this small book fool you. It's a small book that can produce big results when you use the wealth-building secrets I'm about to share with you.

With all that said, let's begin...

Oh – one more thing... If you like this little book, download the Audio Book version from Audible.com – and listen to this book in its original audio format. Listening and reading this book might give you the ultimate motivation to get started and change your life.

With all that said, let's begin…

This is TJ Rohleder. Welcome to part-time wealth. How to make huge sums of money in as little as 90 days!

I'm known as the blue jeans millionaire because I am living proof that anybody can become a millionaire. If that's really what you want to do, or I would even be as bold as to say a billionaire, there's nothing special about me and there's nothing special about all self-made millionaires that I've met and spent time with in many ways you're smarter than they are.

You're probably better looking than they are. You're probably more talented than they are. Look the wealthiest people in the world that started with nothing I'm talking about. Self-made millionaires, self-made billionaires. Ultimately, they got involved in the right opportunities with the right people. Now that's my story. Somewhere along the line in the early to mid-1980s. So I'm dating myself. I'm 63 years old. Somewhere I got this crazy idea that I wanted to become a millionaire. And I had none of the qualities that you would think of that it would take to make millions of dollars. I wasn't born into wealth. I wasn't educated. Some people would say at that time, I had trouble even putting a coherent sentence together.

Yet I had the desire. I really believed that it was possible to make a lot of money. Now, what I found since then is this people that have made millions of dollars starting from scratch or part-time wealth, however much money you want to make. They got involved in the right opportunities with the right people. Why it's possible for you to make huge sums of money in as little as 90 days, you've got to get involved in an opportunity where the amount of money that you make has very little, or in some cases, nothing to do with the amount of time work and effort and energy that you actually put in. The richest people in the world make their money.

The bulk of their money comes from what we call leveraged income. You work an hour; you get paid for an hour. That was the kind of one back in the day when I first got started; I was a welder in a factory making mobile home frames. Before that, I worked construction jobs. Before that, I worked in the oil field in south central Kansas. I dropped out of high school to work in the oil field. That was the mid-1970s at that time. When we had the oil embargo and, I could get a job working on a rig making huge sums of money back then for an uneducated, basically semi illiterate teenager, that was what we call linear income.

You work an hour; you get paid for that hour. That's how most people make their money. And that is the worst way that you can make money because time and energy are limited. The richest people in the world make their money through what's called leveraged income. So they have other people, we call it OPM other people's money, time, and resources that allow them to get paid for things that have very little or even nothing to do with the amount of time work and effort and energy that you put in that they put into it.

Your time is limited. Even if you're a brain surgeon, you can only make so much money per hour. If you're a lawyer that charges $450 an hour. If you want to get wealthy, you have to find a way to make money through leveraged income. Somewhere in the 1980s, I got a wild idea that I was going to become a millionaire.

This is way before the internet, or the worldwide web. Back then, I had to send away for get rich quick programs. I had to join all of these goofy network-marketing companies, no offense, if you're involved in network marketing. That's how I had to get my start, but at least I believe that it was possible. And it's even more possible for you today. That was back in the 1980s. I did bumble around for a few years and I got involved in the wrong things with the wrong people. And I lost a lot of money and the naysayers in my life.

You have to get involved in opportunities where the amount of money that you make has very little or even nothing to do with the amount of time, work, effort, and energy that you put into it. It's a very powerful opportunity because I believe that it was possible to make millions of dollars.

This is real; It's legitimate in every way. It's based on the best of everything we've done to generate millions of dollars for ourselves and our clients.

PART-TIME WEALTH

This is T.J. Rohleder. I want to thank you in advance for taking the time to go over all of this. Chris Lakey and I have been working together for over 25 years. I know about what it takes to turn a small sum of money into a huge and growing fortune. We are presenting the Ascension model; you'll get a good understanding of all of this.

We are looking forward to welcoming you as a member and helping you make the largest amount money. Ascension model is the most proven business model. We've been involved in all kinds of low cost opportunities. People with very limited resources, making a lot of money, not every time, but enough times. We spent many years working with low-cost opportunities where the only people that made a lot of money where the people with a lot of experience, knowledge, skills, and money contacts. Those people will make money, no matter what the opportunity is, if you're a heavy hitter, you can take almost any low-cost business opportunity and potentially make a lot of money. There are all kinds of low-cost opportunities out there. Mostly, network marketing and affiliate type of things, where they always have a few people at the top that are making a lot of money. However, when studying those people, you'll see they're great salespeople.

They're dynamic public speakers. They've been successful previously. They bring a lot of skills and abilities to the Ascension model. We saw people with limited resources, making a lot of money. Therefore, when we decided to do our proprietary turnkey affiliate type of program, the Ascension model was a logical. This does make money for the person with limited resources, as long as they follow a simple system. Then they're dedicated to pursuing. So, this is based on the best of everything that we've done to generate millions of dollars for ourselves and our clients. Ordinary people make massive sums of money and many of these low-cost programs. They don't work for the average person. This gives you the ultimate advantage. You get paid big commissions on sales that we make for you. You're not paid by the amount of time, work, effort, and energy you're putting into it. You're being paid by following our simple system. We're making those sales on your behalf. We are your joint venture, business partners. So the more money we make for ourselves, the more we make for you and on the higher levels.

I'm specially talking about level three, four, and five. You not only get paid for sales that we make for you but you're also paid for the sales that we make for the people placed into your team because we pay big commissions of up to $900 per sale. You're also able to get that amount of money per sale for the deals we're making for the people that are on your team. The amount of money you make has little or nothing to do with the amount of time and work you put in, you don't need a computer or internet access. Although most of you already are online and have computers. You're never going to have to talk to anybody or convince anyone. We provide all of the leads.

You never have to bother your friends and family. You're not only paid on the higher levels. You're paid on the sales that we make for the other people that we place into your team, as long as you are qualified for those higher levels. So, it's a membership Ascension model. It's a long term opportunity. We wanted one program that was going to be the last program that we ever did. The Ascension model was a logical, obvious choice because of our involvement with other companies. We saw millions of dollars being paid out to affiliates. You want to make money and the best opportunity to help you turn small sums of your own money into a huge and growing amount is the essential model. So, you've the potential power to get paid massive commissions, not only on the sales we make for you, but the sales we make for the people we place into your team on those higher levels. You're paid on other things other than your time and the work; it allows you to potentially turn minutes a day into thousands of dollars a month. That is potential, not promised income; read all of our disclaimers. We're in a highly regulated marketplace. If you're ready to get started at any time you can call our assistance. The number is 620-869-7074. You maybe have even talked to one of our representatives who's here to help you on your journey and answer any questions you have.

You've looked at different types of things that could help you make more money and might have led you down a path where you've looked at things like franchises. It might have led you to explore opportunities with certain types of networking marketing. Perhaps, you've looked at starting a local business of some kind. Maybe you even have a local business. We work with many different kinds of people. Maybe part of the reason you're pursuing something different because you are a slave to your business. You become the kind of person that you didn't want to become, where you end up sending hours every day, slaving over your business.

Maybe you have a team of employees that are driving you crazy. You never know, there's all kinds of people that we end up working with because there are a lot of different kinds of people that are looking for a unique way to make more money. We want to encourage you and let you know why we believe our system has those other opportunities beat. A lot of people end up thinking that is, when they think about getting started with something, many times they end up going the direction of a franchise.

The good things is that a franchise gives you a product to sell or a group of products to sell. It gives you some kind of a system. It gives you the support and help that you need. These are good things to have; if you're in business you want those things. But there's also the golden handcuffs, if you will the bad part of a franchises, some of the most proven franchises can cost you hundreds of thousands, if not a million dollars or more just get off the ground. However, they're very expensive. Most people say, I like the idea of a franchise, but I could never afford the kind of startup fee that it costs to get into a franchise, or I don't want to go to a bank and beg for a million dollar loan just to start a franchise.

However, the cost is prohibitive for many people. The second thing, maybe this is even more important for some people, that is that franchises. They come with a lot of rules, restrictions, and ways you can or cannot do business, and they're not very entrepreneurial. They give you a system to plug into, but if you don't do things exactly the way that they say you should do them, they will revoke your franchise license. So, you are bound by all of their restrictions and rules. That's not entrepreneurial. If you're the kind of entrepreneur that likes to go get things done and you have vision all of the qualities that make for a good entrepreneur that doesn't always mesh well with the franchise. So, a lot of people that are entrepreneurial are turned off by the idea of having a franchise with their thumb on them all the time, telling them what they can do and cannot do, but the design of their store, all these details that make it so that an entrepreneurial fuels trapped.

Usually that means they're turned off by that kind of a system or an opportunity, even if a franchise oftentimes comes with the things that you need to be successful.

The problem with network marketing, whether there's few problems. One of the problems with network marketing is that, it pays tiny commissions spread out over large numbers of distributors. In fact, when you read the compensation plans of many network-marketing opportunities, they will tell you the right in their plan, that you can make a lot of money. Here's how we pay commissions. Then you dive in and you find out that because the way they pay, you need to attract thousands of distributors.

You need to have a huge team of

people because you get paid a small commission on each of them, when you build a team, that's got 10 level deeps, and you've got thousands of people never are able to be the type of person that brings in thousands of other distributors. Network marketing is exciting. It sounds good for many people, but the reality is they're never going to be the kind of person that brings in thousands of people. They're not that kind of person. Most people struggle and fail because they don't achieve those kinds of results. Now, the other problem with network marketing is that for many people, it just has, there's kind of a negative feeling about it.

They've heard about network marketing over the years. Maybe they're familiar with Amway or Herbalife, or one of the other multi-billion dollar companies that have been around for a long time, and they've been pitched by their friends and family. All they know about network marketing that's something I got to bug friends and family about, I've got to have meetings and invite people to come to a ballroom somewhere and listen to a pitch. I've got to constantly be bugging my friends and trying to get all the people that I know to join my network marketing deal. That is just kind of a negative turnoff and for good reason who wants to bug their friends and family all the time. Usually, you want to keep business, friends, and family separate those.

One of the things that we are looking at when we built our system is that we wanted to feature some of the highlights and the main benefits of franchises, things like a proven system, a lineup of products and services. In this case, a membership package of several different membership options with an affiliate system that pays big commissions. As you, get the best, and all the help and support you need, so you get some of the benefits of franchise type model. Then some of the benefits of network marketing like the ability to get paid for the efforts of other people, but something that allows you to also get paid big commissions on a small number of sales.

Therefore, you don't have to bring in thousands of people. We're going to go into some mathematical examples. When someone takes just one of our packages, it's kind of a bundled package. It pays a total commission of $1,750. That is a $1,750 commission on one sale that's made for you. We make those sales for you. You don't have to be a super salesperson. You don't have to talk to people on the phone. You don't have to drag people to meetings. You don't have to talk to your friends and family and try to get involved. You don't have to do any of the selling yourself, just let our system and the tools do the selling for you. You get paid when our phone rings. We make the sales for you. So, you don't have to do any of that, but you help us attract those potential members. Our top individual membership is a $900, pays a $900 commission. If someone just purchases that one package, oftentimes when people purchase that they purchase it as part of a bundled package. It includes three of our membership levels all at one time. That pays a onetime commission of $1,750. So, big commissions are possible with small numbers of sales.

One of our representatives who was working with you, if that's the case, you're welcome to call them right back, tell them that you're ready to purchase your membership package. When you call that number, you'll connect with one of TJ's assistant. We're happy to help you with anything you need before you purchase. And of course, they'll help you walk through the order process, get your application processed, and we will get you out a welcome package, and you'll be on your way. We look forward to working with you and having you be an important part of our affiliate team. We're excited to start helping you get paid big commissions on sales that we make for you. You get paid when our phone rings, we do the selling for you. You just have to have the right system.

We're also a nation of laws and we respect that. Therefore, you can't promise or guarantee somebody's going to make $10,000 a month or $50,000 a month or a hundred thousand a month or a hundred thousand a year. It's illegal and immoral to promise and guarantee that somebody's going to make a specific sum of money. Also, there are things that are always outside of our control.

Business is volatile. Therefore, you can't guarantee or promise that anybody's going to make any specific amount of money as a guarantee like this is a sure deal, not even the best franchises, like McDonald's, if you invested in a McDonald's franchise, you'd be virtually guaranteed to make millions of dollars based on historical reference. I think only one McDonald's ever closed because of lack of profitability, only one and that was in the early years. Yet McDonald's in the top franchises, they can't promise or guarantee that you're going to make millions of dollars or any specific sum of money.

Ascension model is the most proven business model. We've been involved in several of them with other companies. We've always seen people with limited resources, make a lot of money, not in every case but enough times that when it came time for us to choosing one business model, that was, going to be the last one that we were ever going to get involved with for ourselves and our clients, friends, family, and members.

The Ascension model was the obvious logical choice. This is powerful pays you big commissions, not only on the sales that we make for you, but on the higher levels of our five level Ascension model. The top three levels of our Ascension model, they not only pay you directly for the sales that we make for you, but they also pay you a bonus commission on the sales that we make for the other people that we have placed into your affiliate team. Now, those people can use the same exact system.

It's a member affiliate program. As they move into one of our higher membership levels, assuming that you yourself are a member of that higher level, you can also get paid those bigger commissions on those additional membership purchases. It's a 100% matching bonus on all of these higher-level memberships that are sold for them. This would be powerful if all this was us paying you a big commission for the sales that we make for the leads that we help you generate, where you don't have to talk to anybody, you don't need a computer, you don't need internet access. We take care of all of that for you. If that's all this opportunity was it would be more than enough and yet getting paid on sales that we make for those higher level packages for the people that we place into your team.

For example, you get a $900 cash commission for every level, four-lifetime membership that we make for you. Assuming that you are a member yourself of level four, but you also get a matching 900 dollars bonus commission. When we make one of those sales for the people on your affiliate team. As long as you're a member of those higher levels, you are going to receive a $900 cash commission. We pay every Thursday by good old-fashioned check, no direct deposits. Every time we make a lifetime level four sale, you're going to get $900, but those people now become part of your affiliate team. They have a chance to use the same system that you're using every time they make, or we make a lifetime level four sale on their behalf, they get the $900 commission, but you also get a matching commission.

If you had just one person that we placed into your affiliate team, that we made 10 of those sales for every month, you would get $9,000 a month in matching bonus commissions. If you had five of those people on your team, that would be $45,000 a month. That's over a thousand dollars a day. What did you have to do to get it? Call this number 620-869-7074. I'm using that example in the literature that $45,000 a month example. I would love it if you could pick up the ball and run with it.

We use examples so that it helps you understand how we pay commissions. By sharing examples with you, you're able to get a better understanding of how you earn money and how we pay commissions and a better understanding of how our compensation plan works and how our matching bonus works and all of these things. It helps us all understand how things work a little better. We can't promise or guarantee that you'll make any specific amount of money. That's not what we're doing, and that would be unethical, immoral, and illegal on top of all of that. However, it's important to you to have an understanding of how you get paid commissions.

There are five membership levels. The first two only one person gets paid a commission. Most of our level one introductory packages, we let our affiliates keep all of the money on those initial orders. That's a hundred percent of the money. Why do we let you keep all of it?

Because we want to reward you for the effort that you engage in to help us attract those customers. We have some turnkey systems for you and some ways that we can help you with that, but basically whether you're doing it yourself, or you're letting us help you as an affiliate, you are helping us attract a potential member and we reward you with those commissions. So on level one, we let you keep all of the money. We do have some introductory offers that do not cost anything, a free report, something like that. So in that case, it's a free, a free inquiry, so just that's how our level one, the introductory offers, if there's a paid level one offer, which several of our introductory offers are, you keep all of that money.

Then on level two, our first membership package, that's where people plug into our affiliate system. It's kind of our entry level into all of the things that we do to help you as an affiliate. It's our primary membership package. We just pay the affiliate that the sale is made for. There's a couple of options for that. There's a one year membership and, also a lifetime. Most people start with a lifetime. If you looked at the form that we sent to you, it just focuses on the lifetime memberships, because that is what most people want to do. They want to set it and forget it, so to speak. So they want to purchase a lifetime membership and just be all in and, fully qualified in everything for life, not to hassle with an annual fee or anything like that, but we do have an annual option.

So if someone takes the annual option or the lifetime option, just the one person gets paid the commission on that. So that commission is paid to the person that we made the sale for. We call that our direct affiliate. If we helped you make that membership sale, for example, the lifetime level two pays a $500 commission, just one person, the person who that sale was made on behalf of the affiliate, the direct affiliate gets paid that direct commission, and then levels three, four, and five. We also have a direct affiliate commission. That's paid to the affiliate, that's you, if you're helping us, and you're the direct affiliate, you get paid the upfront commission, but then we also have a second tier of commission that pays a 100% matching bonus that starts with levels three, four, and five.

Bonus commission pays you, a commission on the sales that we make for the people that are a part of your affiliate team. So, everybody who is a member has access to our members only affiliate system. The way that works is that, once they become a member, they can use our affiliate system just like you, and they can attract members and, and they put themselves in position to get paid commissions, on sales that we make for them. The best word to use to describe it is the sponsor. They're below you, you're above them. This is kind of network marketing kind of language, which is somewhat of a turnoff to us, it's helpful to understand the hierarchy of how things work.

When someone is a part of your team, you're now their sponsor, you're the head, and they're below you on your affiliate team. That's the easiest way to think about it. We pay you a 100% matching bonus on the commissions that we send to them for the sales that we make for them. On levels three,

26

four, and five, the person who is the direct affiliate that got paid, the commission gets paid up front, and then their sponsor gets paid that 100% matching bonus.

It's a $900 direct commission and a $900 matching bonus commission, because those numbers match. If you have someone on your team who is using our system, and we paid them a $900 commission, because they had a level four membership sale that was made for them and you're their sponsor. You're going to get a $900 matching bonus commission. That $900 commission is going to come to you without your direct input or knowledge. You don't have to even be aware that it was happening because we're using the system in helping our affiliates. That includes the people that are on your team. When we make a sale for them, that's going to trigger in our system that in this case, a level four membership sale would be a $900 commission that went to them.

We're going to see that you are their sponsor, and that's going to trigger a $900 bonus commission that goes to you as well. So, that's no matter how many people are on your team, it doesn't matter what the exact commission is. $900 is just an example based on level four. Anytime we send them a commission and you're qualified for it, which means you are a member at that level, you are going to receive that 100% matching bonus. Now, any matching bonus that's not qualified for, it just passes up and passes over the non-qualified person. It passes up to the sponsor who is qualified. So the cool thing about that is that we do pay that commission to someone who is qualified and you could have a team. In fact, only two people get paid, but if you had a team member who was a part of your affiliate team they've used our system and they've sold a membership and someone is using our affiliate system, that's two or three levels below you, technically, you would not normally be qualified for that commission because there's only two people to get paid, but here's where it gets exciting, because if they're not qualified for that commission, it will bypass them and bounce up to you.

If you are qualified, it will stop at you. So you could actually get paid a matching bonus commission on a sale that was made, what you would think of in terms of linear terms, two or three levels below you not like network marketing, but there's just a pass up feature so that you get paid that commission because the people below you who would've otherwise qualified for it were not qualified. So that's a way we reward our members who have taken more action, who are a higher membership level qualifier by giving you the pass up commission that would've otherwise wouldn't somebody else, because they're not qualified for it. So, that's not something we talked about in depth, it is an important part of our system. So you can qualify for those bonus commissions. Even on sales, you didn't even, you weren't actively aware that were even happening.

Based on levels three, four, and five paying that matching bonus, if you just had a small number of people on your affiliate team who were out there making those kinds of sales and let's say you had 10 people on your affiliate team. Those 10 people had each resulted in levels three, four, and five sales that totaled a thousand dollars in commissions. We would send them a thousand dollars each. There are 10 of them. Your commission is 10 times that because you are getting a thousand dollars in bonus commissions for each of those 10 sales that happen that's $10,000 or 10, each those 10 people, not 10 sales, those 10 people each got a thousand dollars in commissions. You would get 10 times.

So your commission from those 10 people and the matching bonus would be $10,000 in that example. So it doesn't take a lot of people. We said before unlike traditional network marketing and some of those things where you have to drag thousands of people in, and you got to get everybody and their uncle to join. You look at their compensation plans and you've got to have tons of people on your team because you're getting paid tiny commissions that are spread out over large numbers of people with this system. It only takes a handful of people to get paid big commissions, not only because of big commissions up front, but the 100% matching bonus pays you on sales we make for other people. And just a small number of those as you've seen, can put big commissions in your pocket.

If you're ready to get started, you can get back to the representative. We've got a few representatives. We don't play games here. We don't have a team of cutthroat salespeople or anything to talk to you. We're pretty low key here. We can help you. The main thing is we want to answer your questions and we want to walk you through this process. So you know exactly what this looks like and how you're, how you fit into this. We'd love to start working with you.

If you go to your five level Ascension model application form, you'll see that there are three different options under step number one. So find your original materials. Usually we put that five level Ascension model membership application form on the last page. Some of you have already received some follow up with that application form, and then you look under step number one, there's only three steps on that application form. Step number one is to enroll in the membership package that you select. So we started with the best, because if you can afford it, it's definitely in your best interest to go with the best option. And that best option qualifies you for life. Now it's the lifetime for all the higher, so it's levels two, three, four, and five.

That is a lifetime qualification. You can do the math yourself and you can work back if you really want to get a timeline here.

This is a long term decision that you're making, and those prices may seem high. You look at that top option, which is a savings of $482. It's still just under $6,000. You're thinking $6,000 you spread it out over a 10 year period or a 20 year period. And you'll see how low it is. This is a willable and a sellable part of your entire estate not to sound morbid but just as part of your estate planning should something happen to you. The money will continue to come in and be it's part of your overall estate. So if you can afford it, go with the top option, get qualified all the way, but if you still have doubts, if you're skeptical, which a lot of people are. If you're not skeptical these days, you're going to get taken advantage of.

It's good to be skeptical. You can always get back with your representative and ultimately that can lead to a call with me. So if you're serious and you're still skeptical, your representative can actually get you an appointment with me. I love the Ascension model. When I say it's the most proven business model we've ever seen in all of these decades that we've been doing this.

We've been involved in several of these with company, the Ascension model has paid out millions of dollars. People have limited resources. If you're confident, and if you can afford it, $5,985 it might be a lot of money to you. It might be a little money to you. It might be a huge risk. It might be a small risk. If you can afford it, go all the way you'll be doing what we call maximizing the complain you'll be making. You'll be making all the money and on those higher levels, you're not only getting paid for the sales we make for you, but you're getting paid for the sales that we make for the people that we put into your team.

That's really important. I'm going to give you a mathematical example here. That's just going to blow you away. It is part of the literature. So you may have already read it. But look, if you have your doubt, start with the lower options and work your way up. That's why we call it the Ascension model. You ascend up, start with the level two, which the lifetime level two, as you'll see is just $997. Spread that out over a 10 year period. You'll see how ridiculously low that price is, but let me leave you now, those of you that have read all the way through, you're just proving to us just how serious you are.

The top three levels of our Ascension

model. They not only pay you directly for the sales that we make for you, but you also get a bonus commission on the sales that we make for the other people that we place into your team. Now, those people can use the same system. As long as you're qualified for those levels, as they move up those higher levels, you get paid up to $900 cash. Every time we make a sale for you, but it's got a hundred percent matching bonus. So you also get a $900 commission for every lifetime level four sale that we make on their behalf. So 10 of those sales that we make for you every month, as an example only again read our disclaimers. We can't promise or guarantee that you're going to make a thousand dollars a day or any specific sum of money.

Nine or ten of those level four sales every month, as long as you're qualified, and you are a level four member yourself 10 of those sales every month, and you're getting $9,000 a month. If that was all there was to it, that would be great. $9,000 a month is awesome. When we're the ones that are making those sales on your behalf, you're never having to talk to anybody. You don't need a computer, you don't need internet access, none of that. But it's got the matching bonus. So if you had one person on your team that was also averaging 10 sales a month, that we're making on their behalf, they're getting the $9,000 a month which is great for them, but you get the a hundred percent matching bonus which means you're also making 9,000 a month, five of those people on your team, as an example only, and you're getting $45,000 a month.

We can't promise or guarantee that no honest or ethical person would ever promise or guarantee that you'd make $45,000 a month or any specific sum, and yet go to try to borrow money from any institution or even your family members. They're going to ask you for a business plan. That includes some kind of an income example or projection of some kind that shows that the potential is there. I promise you the potential is here. You can just call 620-869-7074, but I urge you not to do it. I know you're serious about making money.

So let us help you if you still have doubts and stuff. That's okay. In fact, that's pretty common reach out to your representative or you can even get a call from us.

We appreciate you taking the time to do this and to hang with us for a little bit, get to know our system a little better. I mentioned this earlier there's a benefit to reading.

So we appreciate you being with us. Essentially there are three ways to get started with the membership and you can check out. In fact, on the back of the form, it kind of goes into a brief overview and description of all of the benefits of each membership package. We're not going to go over that here because you can read about it and it will go into those details and, tell you a little more about each of those membership packages.

It is section five that has some more details about each level of membership and how all of that works. So I would refer you to the report for some of those specifics, but

I want to talk about is the three options that you have for getting started today. That is the good, the better and the best.

There's not one package that's perfect for everybody. We're not going to high pressure. That's not what we are about. It's not a game we play. Now we are in business to make a profit, and we certainly appreciate you being a member. We appreciate those of you who want to get started with our all in best package. It certainly helps us.

We appreciate that. As far as our affiliates go, they appreciate a bigger commission when a bigger sale is made. So we are here in business to make a profit and serve our customers and our affiliates. But as far as pressure goes, you're just not going to find that here. That's not what we are all about. In fact, we only want you to purchase the best package if that's what you decide is best for you, and if it's what your budget can afford. And you're the kind of person that wants to start at the top and go all in that best package is the best one for you to choose. There's a reason we call it the best package. Why, because you start at the very top, you start with an all in membership and level five is given to you, the qualification for level five part of our affiliate system is given to you as a free gift.

You read about that because it's a unique, it's not really the same kind of membership that our core memberships at levels two, three, and four have. So it's a unique standalone. And so if you're interested in owning and, receiving level five and being a part of that, you're welcome to join that, but it's kind of a separate animal that exists on its own. So we do qualify you as an affiliate for that is the only level that you will not be a member of unless you choose to add that at some point in the future. Because it's kind of a unique membership package that stands alone. The best package starts you off with levels two, three, and four, and those are lifetime memberships, but it's all in for qualifications.

You're fully qualified as an affiliate, you'll receive all the levels of membership two, three, and four. So you'll receive all access to all of our membership benefits, all of our coaching that goes along with it, everything it's our top package. You get a savings of $482 off that package. We did that just because we wanted to end up with a number for you to get started that ended up being under $6,000. So we decided to give you a little bit extra special savings off of purchasing those separately anyway. You could save $482 if you're ready to go all in with that. That's our best package. Our middle package is just levels two and three.

Those are also both lifetimes, but you will miss out on level four for now. Again, you can always add it later, so there's no worries, no pressure there. If you want to add it in the future, you're welcome to do that. But starting off today with the better package starts you with levels two and three that comes under $2,500 as you can see. Then the good package is a starter. It's where a lot of people end up starting. There's no problem there. You can just get started with level two as a lifetime member for $997 today. So that's an easy place for a lot of people to start. If you have questions about how all this works together, if you have questions about yourself and your abilities to use our system or anything like that, a lot of people just start out with the good package.

They just start out with that level two lifetime membership package. If you are interested and excited about what you've read and you're like, this really does sound like something that I could get behind. And it sounds like something that I could be excited about and something that really can work for me. But you're sitting here today and you're saying I just really don't think that I can swing $997 right now, we do have a way to get you started with a smaller package to get started. So I would say this, it's not in, it's not available on the form that we sent to you, but if you call, if you ask them about how to get started, they can go over those options with you.

You can ask for an appointment with TJ. What they'll do is they'll do a three-way call in to TJ at an appointment time, when he is available and you're available and his representative will patch you together and you'll be on a three-way call. And TJ will speak with you for a few minutes, answer any questions you have. He can go over that lower price option if that's what needs to work for you and your budget and where you're interested in getting started. You're welcome to go over that with him. And he'll be happy to do that. You just have to ask, but most people get started with one of those three options on the form. You're also welcome to mail us or fax us that form. If you want to do that, there's no problem doing that, but you can get started today by just calling right now.

You can get back to the representative. You were already working with. We'll get you connected with the right person who can help you. We don't play games or anything like that, what you might think of as cutthroat salespeople who are all out there scrambling to make sure that they talk to you. We're from Kansas. We're easy going, we're Midwesterners. And we're known for being pretty laid back. So, we don't play games like that. So just give us a call or call your representative back.

We'll connect you with the right person and we'll make sure you get taken care of, okay, that's my promise to you. We'll get you to the right person. No problem. If you have any questions, we want to answer all your questions. We want you to be ready to get started at the package that you choose that's best for you. And we want to help you achieve the success that you're looking for. I think we've got the system that can help you do that. And the way to get started is to plug in with our good, our better, or our best membership package. So again, start at the bottom. There's no shame in that. There's no problem doing that. A lot of people do that get started with just level two, our good package, with just level two, or go ahead and take the better one and add level two and three at the same time.

You can get started at the top, all in with that best membership package. Just take care of it all front levels, two, three, and four. I want to say this as well. I don't know that we've mentioned this, but a lot of people start with the best package, it's more convenient for them to just take care of it all upfront. It is $5,985, and you're saving $482 with that package right off the bat. Some people prefer to just take care of that all front, because it's the easiest there's no hassle, just one time payment and you're done, some people they say, I'm all in this sounds exciting. I want to start out with the best package. However, I can't swing the full $5,985 up front in one payment.

Can I split that into a couple or three payments to fit my budget better? The answer's yes. You just have to ask, we don't know what you're thinking until you tell us what you're thinking, but if you'd like to go all in with that best package, or our better package for that matter, if you like you find the package that fits you best and we'll find a way to make it work. That's not on the form that we sent to you. So you need to call, talk to your representative, let us work with you on that. We'll go over the options. You tell us which package you're thinking about. You tell us which package you're interested in. And then if you say I love the idea of going all in and starting at the top.

The best package is perfect for me. I'm good to go, except I can't swing the full $5,985 today. What can you do to help me? We will go over those options. We've got a few options, something to fit your budget. We will help work that through for you, and you can pay over a couple or three months. We can split that up into monthly payments to fit your budget better. Or if you say, Hey, listen, I want to take care of this in biweekly payments. You don't want to pay, give me a few weeks to pay this off. We'll get you set up and secure your position today, but you can split that into a few payments. Okay? We can go over those options, but you just have to ask, let us know what you're thinking. Cause we can't read your mind, but you let us know where you're at.

You let us know what you're thinking, and we'll find a package or we'll create a package that fits your budget based on these parameters, the good, the better, or the best. If you tell us which package you're interested in and we'll find a way to make that work for you. And I want to say again, either get back to the representative who gave you our phone number to listen to this message. They'll be happy to help you. You can call them back directly. If you don't have their contact information, you lost it or you don't remember who it was or whatever the case may be. You're welcome to just call TJ's assistant Marilyn. And she heads our team and she'll be happy to get you to the right person.

So no worries. You can just call 620-869-7074. She'll be happy to just let her know that you were listening to this message. Let her know that you are interested in, becoming a member and let me know if you're interested in the good, the better or the best package and just kind of let me know what you need. And they'll be happy to get back to you right away and we'll help you get started. And we'll get you to the representative. You need to talk to again, if you need to talk to TJ or you'd like to talk to TJ, just let them know, and they'll get an appointment for you to speak with him for a few minutes as well. But, it's important to call now get started because the first step on the journey is to take the first step.

So you got to get started. And that is where we're at right now. So we appreciate you checking out this report. Appreciate you reading through the report. So if you want to catch it another time you're welcome and anytime you're ready to get started, just talk to your representative or call 620-869-7074. Marilyn will be happy to get you in the right place. So, let me say this by the way just because this does happen.

This number 620-869-7074 is available to you anytime. And it's also the number we'll call you back from we've got it programed. So all of our representatives will be dialing you back from that same phone number. 620-869-7074 is our area code. And that will be where the call comes from. So watch for that phone call when we call you back, make sure you answer, keep your phone with you.

Most of us are using cell phones these days, not too many office landlines, even businesses mostly use cell phones these days. Unless you're calling from a landline where you can't get a call back, if you're out on the road keep your phone handy, give us a cell phone number we can get back to you with, and then watch for a call from area code. If you want to go ahead and program that phone number into your phone book, or into your contact list as TJ. That's great. Lets you know that TJ's the one calling you back or one of his representatives. But that way when the phone rings you'll know it's us either way, watch for phone number, watch for area code.

So make sure you answer when we call you back. I just wanted to end with that. So thank you so much again for reading. We'll let you go. Appreciate you hanging out with us today and get back to your representative or call again 620-869-7074. We would love to take your questions. We'd love to talk to you about getting started. Your future's on the line. I know you're looking for an opportunity because you listened this far. So take the next step. Let's start working together. Have a good one. And we'll talk to you soon.

Thank you for reading this book. We hope that we've more than made up for in sincerity. This is a real opportunity in every way. In order to get wealthy, you have to do what the wealthy people are doing. We've done to generate millions of dollars for ourselves and our clients. There is nothing special about us. If we can do it, anybody can do it. You can also reach out to me personally, go to www.heytj.com. That's my online support. If you want to talk about this idea. You can go to this website www.heytj.com or you can send an email to tickets@heytj.com and put part-time wealth in the subject matter. You can request a copy of the Part-Time Cash Report. You can ask any question you want, and I will personally answer your question so that it really will be a two-way communication between you and us and keeping in line with the spirit.

Again, remember the richest people, as I said in the beginning are no different from you. They got involved in the right opportunities with the right people. The money that they make is based on leveraged income, not linear income, where the amount of money they make has little or nothing to do with the amount of time, work, effort, and energy that they actually put in. That's the opportunity that you'll have when you get involved with us in our five level Ascension model, which has been at the heart and soul of what we've talked about. I hope you'll get convinced so that you can make a more educated, intelligent, objective decision about whether you want to get involved with us or not, by at least sending for that part-time cash report and finding out what all of this is really about.

A lot of things that it didn't mean

when I first got started back in the 1980s, now wealth covers the subject of wealth in all aspects of life, however much money you want to make. It's out there for you, whatever your dreams are, they're out there for you. Don't let the naysayers crush those dreams, reach out to me and let's start a real conversation. That's more than just a one way conversation with you asking me all the questions that I can help answer or I'll do my best to help answer. So thank you, God bless you. I'll look forward to hearing from you.

PROLOGUE

Be sure to check out the audio book on Audible.com. This book is a written transcript of an audio conversation. Take a Guru to Lunch was founded on the premise that we were having a conversation over lunch. But in order for this to be a real conversation, you need to add your comments. Please reach out through our support desk and let me know what you think. Connect through <u>tickets@heytj.com</u> and mention this Part-Time Wealth book in the subject line. Because I want to have a real conversation with you, I personally answer all messages. I look forward to hearing from you soon.